S0-AFB-664

STATES

SOUTH CAROLINA

A MyReportLinks.com Book

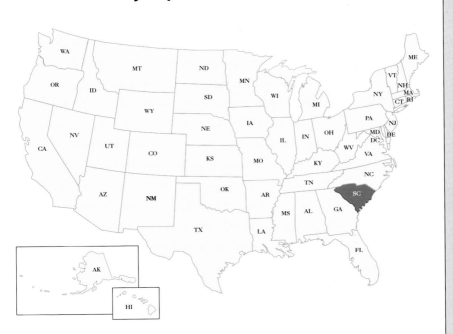

Vikki L. Berri

MyReportLinks.com Books

an imprint of

Enslow Publishers, Inc.

Box 398, 40 Industrial Road
Berkeley Heights, NJ 07922
USA

J975.7
BERRI
07/04

MyReportLinks.com Books, an imprint of Enslow Publishers, Inc. MyReportLinks is
a trademark of Enslow Publishers, Inc.

Library of Congress Cataloging-in-Publication Data

Berri, Victoria L.
  South Carolina / Victoria L. Berri.
      p. cm. — (States)
Includes bibliographical references (p.) and index.
Summary: Discusses the land and climate, economy, government, and
history of the Palmetto State. Includes Internet links to Web sites
related to South Carolina.
  ISBN 0-7660-5139-0
  1. South Carolina—Juvenile literature. [1. South Carolina.] I.
Title. II. States (Series : Berkeley Heights, N.J.)
  F269.3 .B47 2003
  975.7—dc21

                              2002153582

Printed in the United States of America

10 9 8 7 6 5 4 3 2 1

To Our Readers:
Through the purchase of this book, you and your library gain access to the Report Links that specifically back
up this book.
The Publisher will provide access to the Report Links that back up this book and will keep these Report Links
up to date on **www.myreportlinks.com** for three years from the book's first publication date.
We have done our best to make sure all Internet addresses in this book were active and appropriate when we
went to press. However, the author and the Publisher have no control over, and assume no liability for, the
material available on those Internet sites or on other Web sites they may link to.
The usage of the MyReportLinks.com Books Web site is subject to the terms and conditions stated on the
Usage Policy Statement on **www.myreportlinks.com**.
A password may be required to access the Report Links that back up this book. The password is found on the
bottom of page 4 of this book.
Any comments or suggestions can be sent by e-mail to comments@myreportlinks.com or to the address on
the back cover.

Photo Credits: ArtToday.com, p. 16; © Corel Corporation, p. 3; © 2001 Robesus, Inc., p. 10; © 2003
Friends of the Hunley, p. 41; © 2003 SCI Way, LLC, pp. 31, 32, 36; Enslow Publishers, Inc., pp. 1,
20, 24; Kershaw County Chamber of Commerce and Visitors Center, p. 26; Library of Congress, p. 3
(Constitution); MyReportLinks.com Books, p. 4; National Oceanic and Atmospheric Administration
(NOAA)/Richard B. Mieremet, p. 18; NOAA/Rich Bourgerie, p. 11; NOAA/Sean Linehan, p. 43;
NOAA/William B. Folsom; Photos.com, p. 25; National Park Service, p. 39; Rainbow/PUSH
Coalition, p. 14; South Carolina Department of Parks Recreation and Tourism, pp. 22, 29; South
Carolina State Museum, p. 34; Strom Thurmond Institute/Clemson University, p. 30.

Cover Credit: South Carolina Department of Parks, Recreation, and Tourism

Cover Photo: South Carolina State House in Columbia, South Carolina.

Contents

MyReportLinks.com Books
Great Books, Great Links, Great for Research!

MyReportLinks.com Books present the information you need to learn about your report subject. In addition, they show you where to go on the Internet for more information. The pre-evaluated Report Links that back up this book are kept up to date on **www.myreportlinks.com**. With the purchase of a MyReportLinks.com Books title, you and your library gain access to the Report Links that specifically back up that book. The Report Links save hours of research time and link to dozens—even hundreds—of Web sites, source documents, and photos related to your report topic.

Please see "To Our Readers" on the Copyright page for important information about this book, the MyReportLinks.com Books Web site, and the Report Links that back up this book.

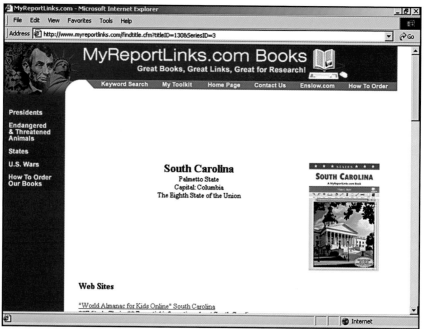

Access:

The Publisher will provide access to the Report Links that back up this book and will try to keep these Report Links up to date on our Web site for three years from the book's first publication date. Please enter **SSC9214** if asked for a password.

Report Links

 The Internet sites described below can be accessed at
http://www.myreportlinks.com

*EDITOR'S CHOICE

▶ **The *World Almanac for Kids Online*: South Carolina**
The *World Almanac for Kids Online* Web site provides a comprehensive
overview of South Carolina's geography, demographics, culture, history,
economy, and government.

Link to this Internet site from http://www.myreportlinks.com

*EDITOR'S CHOICE

▶ **Explore the States: South Carolina**
America's Story from America's Library, a Library of Congress Web site,
tells the story of South Carolina. Here you will read interesting facts
about the state and learn about some South Carolina traditions.

Link to this Internet site from http://www.myreportlinks.com

*EDITOR'S CHOICE

▶ **U.S. Census Bureau: South Carolina**
The U.S. Census Bureau provides statistics on South Carolina. Here
you will find data on people, business, and geography. Click on
"Browse more data sets for South Carolina" to get more information.

Link to this Internet site from http://www.myreportlinks.com

*EDITOR'S CHOICE

▶ **Perry-Castañeda Library Map Collection:
South Carolina Maps**
At the Perry-Castañeda Library Map Collection Web site you can view
historical maps, state maps, and maps of national monuments, parks,
and historic sites.

Link to this Internet site from http://www.myreportlinks.com

*EDITOR'S CHOICE

▶ **South Carolina State Museum**
At the South Carolina State Museum Web site you can explore some
of their online exhibits. Some exhibits include topics such as natural
history, cultural history, science and technology, and conservation.

Link to this Internet site from http://www.myreportlinks.com

*EDITOR'S CHOICE

▶ **The South Carolina Historical Society**
The South Carolina Historical Society's Web site provides a variety
of online resources and exhibits that capture the history of the state.
See the section on online resources, which provides virtual displays
and exhibits.

Link to this Internet site from http://www.myreportlinks.com

 The Internet sites described below can be accessed at
http://www.myreportlinks.com

▶**Andrew Jackson: The Roughshod President**
The American Presidency Web site provides a comprehensive biography of
Andrew Jackson, who was born in Waxhaw, South Carolina. Here you will
learn about his life before, during, and after his presidency.

Link to this Internet site from http://www.myreportlinks.com

▶**Carolina Living**
Carolina Living explores life and lifestyle in the Carolinas by introducing
the cuisine, hobbies, and pastimes of the area. You will also find many local
recipes, personal stories, and regional information.

Link to this Internet site from http://www.myreportlinks.com

▶**Charleston Surrenders**
Learn about the surrender of Charleston to General Alexander Schimmelfennig
on February 18, 1865. This happened during the Civil War.

Link to this Internet site from http://www.myreportlinks.com

▶**The Citadel**
At the official Web site of the Citadel, one of the most prestigious military
schools in the nation, you will find its history and facts about the school.

Link to this Internet site from http://www.myreportlinks.com

▶**Colonial Charters, Grants, and Related Documents**
At the Avalon Project at Yale Law School Web site you can read the South
Carolina constitutions of 1776 and 1778.

Link to this Internet site from http://www.myreportlinks.com

▶**Columbia, South Carolina**
On this site you can learn about the city of Columbia, the state capital of
South Carolina.

Link to this Internet site from http://www.myreportlinks.com

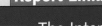
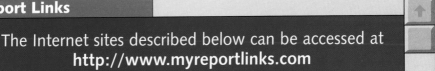

The Internet sites described below can be accessed at
http://www.myreportlinks.com

▶ **Cowpens National Battlefield**
The National Park Service Web site provides a brief description
of Cowpens Battlefield where battles were waged in the southern
campaign of the American Revolution. Click on "InDepth" to learn
more about this historic park.

Link to this Internet site from http://www.myreportlinks.com

▶ **Drayton Hall**
At this Web site you can take a virtual tour of this historic South
Carolina plantation, Drayton Hall. You can also read about Drayton
Hall's history, architecture, land, and much more.

Link to this Internet site from http://www.myreportlinks.com

▶ **Fort Sumter National Monument**
From the National Park Service Web site you can visit Fort Sumter,
located in Charleston Harbor, South Carolina. Click on "InDepth"
to learn more about this historic place.

Link to this Internet site from http://www.myreportlinks.com

▶ **Friends of the *Hunley***
At the Friends of the *Hunley* Web site you will learn about the world's
first submarine, which disappeared off the shores of South Carolina
after successful completion of its first mission during the Civil War.
The site presents the history and discovery of this historic vessel.

Link to this Internet site from http://www.myreportlinks.com

▶ **Jesse Jackson**
Jesse Jackson was born in Greenville, South Carolina. This Web site
contains a brief biography, as well as the details of his accomplishments
as a political and religious leader.

Link to this Internet site from http://www.myreportlinks.com

▶ **Netstate: South Carolina**
NetState provides a basic introduction to South Carolina. Here you
will learn about the state's geography, history, symbols, and people.
You will also find an almanac that contains statistics regarding weather,
facts, and other information.

Link to this Internet site from http://www.myreportlinks.com

Back	Forward	Stop	Review	Home	Explore	Favorites	History

Report Links

 The Internet sites described below can be accessed at
http://www.myreportlinks.com

▶**Ninety Six**
At the National Park Service Web site you can learn about Ninety Six
National Park located in Ninety Six, South Carolina. Here you will find
a brief description of the park's historical significance. Click on "InDepth"
to learn more.

Link to this Internet site from http://www.myreportlinks.com

▶**The Palmetto Experience**
The Palmetto Experience Web site allows you to take an interactive tour of
South Carolina's history. Here you can view maps, time lines, and images.

Link to this Internet site from http://www.myreportlinks.com

▶**River Conservation Program**
At the River Conservation Program Web site you can learn all about rivers
in South Carolina. Here you can take a tour of the rivers and learn about
projects and conservation efforts.

Link to this Internet site from http://www.myreportlinks.com

▶**Santa Elena Homepage**
When the French established Charlesfort in 1562, they became the first
Europeans to settle South Carolina. The Santa Elena Homepage Web site
presents important historical and archaeological information about Charlesfort
and Santa Elena.

Link to this Internet site from http://www.myreportlinks.com

▶**South Carolina**
At the official South Carolina tourism Web site you can explore many regions
in the state. Click on "What to Do" to explore state parks, mountains,
beaches, arts and entertainment, and other activities. You will also find state
facts and learn about the history of South Carolina.

Link to this Internet site from http://www.myreportlinks.com

▶**South Carolina African American History Online**
At the South Carolina African American History Online Web site you
will find biographical sketches about important African Americans from
South Carolina.

Link to this Internet site from http://www.myreportlinks.com

Report Links

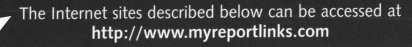

The Internet sites described below can be accessed at
http://www.myreportlinks.com

▶ South Carolina Civil War Battles

At the American Civil War Web site you will find a cartographic guide
(a guide in the shape of a map) to Civil War battles fought in South
Carolina. A description, statistics, and information about each battle
are provided through a linked page.

Link to this Internet site from http://www.myreportlinks.com

▶ South Carolina National Heritage Corridor

Developed to encourage tourism in the South Carolina's rural areas,
this site provides a unique glimpse at the heritage of the state through
virtual backroad tours.

Link to this Internet site from http://www.myreportlinks.com

▶ South Carolina Reference Room

From the South Carolina State Library Web site you can explore many
aspects of the state, including its history, cities, government, education,
and much more.

Link to this Internet site from http://www.myreportlinks.com

▶ South Carolina State

This Web site presents a comprehensive list of facts about South
Carolina along with links to additional information on each fact.
Learn about the state symbols, capital, constitution, flags, maps,
and even the state song.

Link to this Internet site from http://www.myreportlinks.com

▶ Stately Knowledge: South Carolina

The Internet Public Library Web site provides basic facts about South
Carolina. You will also find additional links to Internet resources about
South Carolina.

Link to this Internet site from http://www.myreportlinks.com

▶ We Shall Overcome

From this National Park Service Web site you can explore historic
places from the civil rights movement: including South Carolina
College; Orangeburg, South Carolina; and Columbia, South Carolina.

Link to this Internet site from http://www.myreportlinks.com

South Carolina Facts

▶ **Gained Statehood**
May 23, 1788, the eighth state.

▶ **Capital**
Columbia

▶ **Counties**
46

▶ **Bird**
Carolina wren

▶ **Insects**
Carolina mantid
Tiger swallowtail butterfly

▶ **Flower**
Carolina yellow jessamine

▶ **Gem**
Amethyst

▶ **Tree**
Palmetto

▶ **Fish**
Striped bass

▶ **Songs**
"Carolina" (words by Henry Timrod, music by Anne Custis Burgess)
"South Carolina on My Mind" (words and music by Hank Martin and Buzz Arledge)

▶ **Mottos**
Dum Spiro Spero (Latin for "While I breathe, I hope");
Animis Opibusque Parati (Latin for "Ready in soul and resources")

▶ **Population**
4,012,012*

▶ **Nickname**
Palmetto State

▶ **Reptile**
Loggerhead sea turtle

▶ **Flag**
In the upper left-hand corner on a blue field, is a white crescent matching the ones worn on the caps of South Carolinian troops during the Revolutionary War. In the center of the flag, is a white Palmetto tree representing the heroic defense of the palmetto-log fort on Sullivan's Island during an attack by the British fleet during the Revolutionary War.

Population reflects the 2000 census.

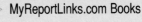
The Palmetto State

South Carolina, the Palmetto State, is located in the southeastern part of the United States. It has a population of about 4 million, making it the twenty-fifth largest state in the Union.[1] The state is sandwiched between North Carolina to the north and Georgia to the south and west. The Atlantic Ocean borders South Carolina on the east.

In the 2000 census, four South Carolina cities: Columbia, Charleston, North Charleston, and Greenville, boasted more than fifty thousand people. Columbia, the capital, is the largest, with over 116,000 people.

The state of South Carolina is shaped like a leaf and got its nickname, the Palmetto State, from the battle of Fort Moultrie. Before the battle of Fort Moultrie in the mid-1700s, the South Carolinians built a fort on Sullivan's Island out of palmetto logs. When the English

▲ Charleston, South Carolina, once called Charles Town, was moved to its present site from across the Ashley River in 1690, twenty years after the city was established. Its name was changed to Charleston in 1783.

attacked this fort, it did not fall. The South Carolinians won this battle and later nicknamed the state after the trees.

South Carolina has much to offer the visitor. Millions come to swim, surf, bike, and hike. People also come for the fairs. One of the state's most popular fairs is the annual Apple Festival. It is held during Labor Day weekend and draws thousands of visitors to the state. The Apple Festival celebrates the beginning of the apple harvest season in Oconee County.

▷ Interesting Places to Visit

Many interesting places in South Carolina are tied to the state's lively history. Fort Sumter, located in Charleston, is where the first shots of the Civil War were fired. Visitors heading for the fort leave Charleston by boat.

When people come to the Palmetto State for the first time, they often start their visit at Charleston. Several of the state's beautiful plantations are located in Charleston. The Boone Hall plantation, a large estate, depicts life in South Carolina in the days before the Civil War. Today, the plantation thrives. It produces commercial crops, serves as the backdrop for major motion pictures, and sponsors events that entertain and benefit visitors and residents of the area.[2] Drayton Hall is also well known because it survived an attack by the Union troops during the Civil War. The attack was foiled because John Drayton, the owner, told the soldiers the house was being used as a hospital for smallpox victims. The soldiers fled the scene.

Charleston is not the only city to have plantation homes. Hopsewee Plantation is located near Georgetown along the Santee River. Hampton Plantation is also on the Santee River. George Washington visited this plantation.

Rock Hill has a plantation called the "White House." These plantation homes are open for tours.

In addition to the historical sites and plantations, people come to South Carolina to swim and surf in the beautiful ocean along the Carolina coastline. One of the most popular areas in South Carolina is the Grand Strand. Some of the finest beaches in the nation are located along this 60-mile stretch of U.S. Highway 17. The Grand Strand is made up of several towns: including Cherry Grove Beach, Ocean Drive Beach, Crescent Beach, and Windy Hill Beach. Murrels Inlet is also part of the Grand Strand. It is known for its seafood restaurants. Visitors also stay at the popular resort, Myrtle Beach.

Georgetown is a popular shopping spot. In the early days, this was the shipping port for the state's resources— rice, cotton, and indigo. Today, the port has been transformed into a Harbor Walkway. It houses a number

▲ Folly Island is located off the coast of South Carolina. It has become a popular vacation alternative to Charleston.

of shops and restaurants. Georgetown is also the home of the Rice Museum. The Rice Museum tells the story of how the plant was important to the growth of the South Carolina colony.

The Blue Ridge Mountains are another popular spot for tourists. People go to the mountains to camp, fish, hike, and raft. One of the Blue Ridge Mountains is said to look like a head. It is named "Caesar's Head." Some say the mountain was named for Roman emperor Julius Caesar while others say it was named after a dog named Caesar.

In addition, South Carolina has been the locale for many popular movies such as *The Abyss, Days of Thunder, Die Hard with a Vengeance, Forrest Gump, Last Dance, The Prince of Tides,* and *That Darn Cat.*

▷ Politics

One of the most famous politicians from South Carolina is Strom Thurmond. He was the oldest and the longest-serving senator in history. He retired in 2003 at the age of one hundred, and died on June 26, 2003.

Rev. Jesse Jackson, a famous African-American minister

and civil rights activist, was born in Greenville, South Carolina, in 1941. After attending the University of Illinois, he went to North Carolina Agricultural and

◁ *Jesse Jackson, a religious leader and human rights activist, was born in Greenville, South Carolina. In 1993, he was awarded the Dr. Martin Luther King, Jr., nonviolent peace prize.*

Technical College. He continued onto Chicago Theological Seminary, where he became a civil rights leader.

President Andrew Jackson was born in the Waxhaws area near the border between North and South Carolina on March 15, 1767.[3] Jackson was the seventh president of the United States and became a national hero during the War of 1812. He was also a congressman, a U.S. Senator, and judge on the Tennessee Supreme Court.

James Francis Byrnes was a Supreme Court justice. Byrnes was also a statesman, jurist, diplomat, congressman, senator, governor, secretary of state, and considered the most distinguished Carolinian of his time.[4]

John Caldwell Calhoun was a public official and political leader. Thomas Heywood was a soldier, patriot, and politician. Ernest "Fritz" Hollings was a politician. Henry Laurens was a political leader.

▷ Other Famous South Carolinians

In addition to politicians, South Carolina has also been home to writers, actors, and baseball players. Alice Childress is a novelist and playwright from Charleston. In 1952, Childress became the first African-American woman to have a play produced in America. Pat Conroy is another popular writer. His novels are set in South Carolina. Peggy Parrish is a children's writer from South Carolina.

Eartha Kitt and Andie MacDowell are famous entertainers from South Carolina. Eartha Kitt is known for her singing and Andie MacDowell did films which included *Groundhog Day* and *Four Weddings and a Funeral.*

Baseball giants "Shoeless Joe" Jackson, Jim Rice, and Lawrence Doby were born in South Carolina. Doby was the first African-American player in baseball's American League. He joined the Cleveland Indians in 1947.

Chapter 2

Land and Climate

South Carolina falls easily into three natural regions. In the northwest corner is the Blue Ridge Region. The rest of the north, and western parts of the state are known as the Piedmont Region. Most of South Carolina is part of the Atlantic Coastal Plain. South Carolinians refer to the Coastal Plain as the Low Country and the Piedmont and the Blue Ridge regions as the Up Country.

▶ Atlantic Coastal Plain

The Atlantic Coastal Plain is split into two parts— the Inner Coastal Plain and the Outer Coastal Plain.

▲ *The Audubon Swamp Garden is located on the Atlantic Coastal Plain. This wildlife preserve is home to many birds, mammals, and reptiles, as well as hundreds of species of plants and flowers.*

The Inner Coastal Plain consists of rolling hills that extend inland from the coast for about seventy miles. The Outer Coastal Plain is the area that is located along the coast. This area is flat, swampy, and broken by many rivers and streams. The Fall Line, which is located at the inner edge of the Coastal Plain, separates the Coastal Plain from the Piedmont.

The Atlantic Coastal Plain extends from the Atlantic Ocean to the western part of the state, covering two-thirds of South Carolina. It runs from the southeast to the northwest. Along the coast, lie the Sea Islands. These islands are small and marshy.

The Piedmont

The Piedmont takes in the rolling plains of the northwestern part of the state. The most fertile soils are found here. When the soil gets wet, it turns into a dark peat or muck, which is good for growing. The Pine Barrens, a forested area, is located in the central Atlantic Coastal Plain.

An upland area, the Piedmont rises gradually north-westward from 400 to 1,200 feet above sea level near the Fall Line, to 1,400 feet along the northwestern edge.[1] When manufacturing took over as the leading economic industry in the twentieth-century, crop production decreased in the Lower Piedmont area. The Lower Piedmont area turned into forests and pastures when the cotton growing industry slowed down. Manufacturing companies moved into the Upper Piedmont area.

Blue Ridge Region

The Blue Ridge region extends from southern Pennsylvania south to Georgia. The Blue Ridge Mountains in South Carolina are lower and less rugged than the

mountains in North Carolina. The forest-covered Blue Ridge Mountains of South Carolina rarely exceed 3,000 feet above sea level. The highest point in South Carolina, Sassafras Mountain, reaches 3,560 feet above the sea.

▷ Rivers

There are three major rivers in South Carolina. They are the Santee, Great Pee Dee, and Savannah rivers. The Santee River, 230 km (143 miles) long, is joined by two other rivers—the Wateree River (Catawba River as it is called in the upper reaches) and the Congaree River. The combination of the two rivers makes the Santee River the longest river in the state. The Congaree River is made up of two rivers as well—the Broad River and the Saluda River. The Great Pee Dee River is also comprised of two

△ This aerial shot allows you to see some of the rivers that dot South Carolina's landscape.

rivers to make it one large river. The two rivers that make up the Great Pee Dee are the Lynches and Little Pee Dee rivers. The Seneca and Tugaloo rivers in northwestern South Carolina combine to form the Savannah River. Together, the Tugaloo and Chattooga rivers form most of the South Carolina-Georgia state line.

With an area of 31,189 square miles South Carolina ranks fortieth among the states in area. This includes 1,006 square miles of inland water and 72 square miles of coastal waters. Running from east to west, the maximum distance, is 273 miles and going from north to south, its maximum extent is 219 miles.

Climate

Hot summers and mild winters characterize South Carolina's climate. The climate of South Carolina is humid. The humid climate comes from the combination of the state's relatively low latitude, the low elevation, the closeness of the warm Gulf Stream in the Atlantic, and the Appalachian Mountains. The Appalachian Mountains help block cold air from coming in from the west.

In January, the average temperature of Charleston is about 48.5°F. The average temperature of Charleston in July is about 80°F. The city, Greer, in the Piedmont Plateau region, has a mean January temperature of about 42.5°F and in July temperature of about 78.5°F.

South Carolina's temperature has ranged from –19°F to 111°F. The record low occurred in 1977 at Caesars Head. The City of Camden, in the north-central part of the state, had the highest temperature ever recorded in South Carolina. On June 28, 1954, the temperature reached 111°F. This matched the 111°F reached at Blackville, South Carolina, in 1925.[2]

NORTH
CAROLINA

BLUE RIDGE

Kings Mtn.
Cowpens Nat'l
Battle Field

1,083 ft.
Sasafrass Mtn.

Greer

Rock
Hill

Greenville

Seneca R.

Saluda R.

Broad R.

Catawba R.

PIEDMONT PLATEAU

Pee Dee R.

Lynches R.

Florence

Marion

Fishing
Cr. Res.

Camden

PINE
BARRENS

Wateree R.

Calhoun
Falls

Lake
Greenwood

Columbia

Lake
Murray

Congaree R.

SAND HILLS

Great
Pee Dee R.

Myrtle
Beach

Strom
Thurmond
Lake

Santee R.

Georgetown

Savannah R.

COASTAL PLAIN

Lake
Marion

Orangeburg

Blackville

Lake
Moultrie

Ashley R.

North
Charleston

Charleston

Sullivan's
Island

GEORGIA

Folly
Island

ATLANTIC
OCEAN

Savannah R.

Beaufort

Parris Island

Hilton
Head
Island

A map of South Carolina.

Rainfall generally happens in late winter and again in summer. Annual rainfall is about forty-five inches in most parts of the state. However, the mountainous north-west area receives up to about seventy inches of rainfall. Snowfall is rare, but does occur in the Blue Ridge Region. Sometimes tornadoes and hurricanes attack the state and cause massive damage. In 1989, Hurricane Hugo struck South Carolina, killing twenty-six and causing over $5 billion in damage.

Tools   Search   Notes   Discuss   Go!

Plant and Animal Life

At one time, forests covered most of South Carolina. Today, more than 60 percent of the state is forest and woodland. Forests on the Atlantic Coastal Plain are especially rich in several types of pine, chiefly longleaf, short leaf, slash, loblolly, and Virginia. They are part of the large Southeastern Pine Forest of the United States. The pines grow on the better-drained lands back from the rivers, as do oak, sweet gum, hickory, magnolia, and other broadleaf trees. Forests of cypress, tupelo, tulip tree, sweet gum, and other species grow in wet areas. Other trees include a palm, the palmetto, which grows mainly along the coast. Oak trees are especially common in the Piedmont Plateau region—along with beech, maple, loblolly, short leaf, Virginia, and pitch pine. In the Blue Ridge Region the forests are composed mainly of oak. Common wildflowers of South Carolina include azalea, gentian, mountain laurel, violet, and yellow jessamine, the state flower.

Vast numbers of white-tailed deer, opossum, rabbit, and raccoon reside in South Carolina. Migrating waterfowl, especially ducks and geese, follow the Atlantic coast, and many kinds of birds, such as the catbird, mockingbird, oriole, and wren, live in the interior regions of the state. Common fish living in South Carolina's rivers and lakes include bass, carp, crappie, and trout. Coastal marine waters contain clams, oysters, shrimp, crab, and others.

Minerals

South Carolina is the only gold-producing state east of the Mississippi River. The state's mineral resources also include vermiculite, which is used for insulation and as a

▲ *The Palmetto tree is the state tree.*

additive for soil; beds of sand, particularly in the Sand Hills; and kaolin, a type of white clay found in the inner Coastal Plain. In addition, the state has deposits of gravel, stone, peat, mica, and gemstones.

South Carolina's mild climate, its Atlantic coast, and its mountains offer fine conditions for swimming, fishing, boating, hunting, golfing, tennis, and other sports. The Grand Strand, a long sand beach with Myrtle Beach as its hub, is one of the main summer recreational centers of the state. Hilton Head Island is known for its many tennis courts and other sports facilities.

Economy

The South Carolina economy achieved its second-best year in the state's history in the year 2000. Business boomed as new businesses and foreign investors moved into the state. Employment and average personal income rose slightly higher than the national average. The state has a lower cost of living than most other states.

In the 1970s and 1980s, South Carolina experienced economic growth similar to other Sunbelt states (the states in the Southeast). South Carolina's low tax rates and large nonunion work force have attracted many firms from the other states as well as foreign countries.

▷ Growth Industries

The service and trade industries were the state's number one moneymakers and leading employers by 2000. Still, farming, food, fiber, and forestry rank near the top of the industries generating income for the state. The farming industry brings in an average of $1.5 billion a year. The food, fiber, and forestry industry provides 460,000 full and part-time jobs, $15.1 billion in income, and creates $35.7 billion in gross sales.[1] Service and trade industries such as finance, insurance, real estate, transportation, and public utilities have been successful.

The rest of the United States—and the world—has long thought of South Carolina as a poor land. The South Carolinians, though, have been aggressively trying to change this image by creating new jobs and spawning new industries. Throughout the years, the South Carolina

economy has seen many changes and will continue to change.

Agriculture/Farming

Despite the recent decline in farming, South Carolina still ranks near the top in the production of several agricultural products. The farms produce apples, peaches, tobacco, cotton, eggs, milk, soybeans, tomatoes, and watermelon. The farms are also ranked high in production of livestock such as cattle, turkeys, and hogs.

In 2001, the state ranked third in peach production, second in flue-cured tobacco, fifth in tomato production, eighth in watermelon production, and ninth in turkeys raised.[2] Farm productivity in South Carolina, as measured by average yield per acre of land, is near the national average in most crops. Tobacco and cotton recorded yields about 11 percent above the national average.[3]

Forestry and Timber

Two thirds of South Carolina is covered in forests. The timber and lumber are used to make paper and paper products. Timber is the number one cash crop

Agriculture is an important part of South Carolina's economy. It is estimated that there are twenty-four thousand farms in South Carolina, covering about 4,700,000 acres of the state.

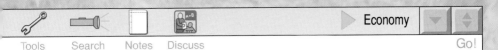

for a majority of South Carolina's counties. The forestry industry employs over thirty-five thousand people. There are over 12 million acres of forestland throughout the state, nearly 72 percent privately owned.[4]

South Carolina's forestry and wood products industry is valued at $7.5 billion a year. It is the third largest manufacturing industry in the state, employing about twenty-six thousand people with a payroll of $8.68 million a year.[5]

Fishing and Hunting

Fishing is another big money maker for the state. Many visitors come to South Carolina to enjoy the fishing and hunting. About 985,000 thousand people—almost 1 in every 3 residents—fishes in South Carolina in some form or fashion. About 300,000 people—roughly one tenth of

▲ Although it has declined in importance, tobacco is still one of South Carolina's main cash crops.

25

the state's population—hunt. In addition, about 807,000 citizens of the state, as well as over 400,000 nonresidents, engage in activities such as bird feeding, bird watching, canoeing, hiking, and backpacking.[6]

▷ Tourism

Tourism is an increasingly important industry in the state. More than three fourths the vacation spending is at Charleston and the resorts of Myrtle Beach and Hilton Head Island. Other major attractions are the Cowpens National Battlefield and Fort Sumter and Kings Mountain military sites.

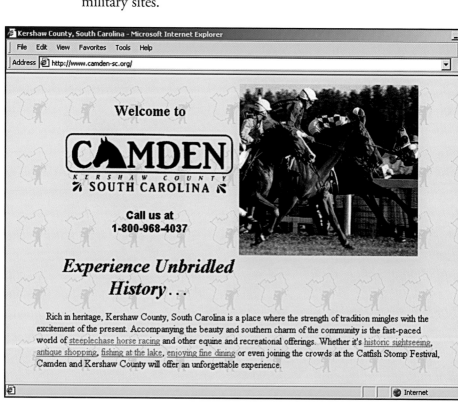

Kershaw County, South Carolina - Microsoft Internet Explorer

File Edit View Favorites Tools Help

Address ⬚ http://www.camden-sc.org/

Welcome to

CAMDEN
KERSHAW COUNTY
🐾 SOUTH CAROLINA 🐾

Call us at
1-800-968-4037

Experience Unbridled History . . .

Rich in heritage, Kershaw County, South Carolina is a place where the strength of tradition mingles with the excitement of the present. Accompanying the beauty and southern charm of the community is the fast-paced world of steeplechase horse racing and other equine and recreational offerings. Whether it's historic sightseeing, antique shopping, fishing at the lake, enjoying fine dining or even joining the crowds at the Catfish Stomp Festival, Camden and Kershaw County will offer an unforgettable experience.

⬚   🌐 Internet

▲ *Steeplechase horse racing is a popular sport in South Carolina. Thousands of fans come to watch this event and enjoy an afternoon of picnics and pony rides.*

Other areas of tourism are the nature sites. Visitors come for the natural habitats of the state. They like to fish and hunt on their vacations. They like to hike and bike through the forests.

Manufacturing

The textile industry became South Carolina's leading business in the late 1800s. Boll weevils ruined cotton crops during the 1920s causing the cotton industry to decline. Although cotton remained the largest crop, the farmers began planting tobacco, soybeans, wheat, and fruits. The Great Depression (1929–39) hurt South Carolina as mills closed and prices for crops dropped.

One of South Carolina's principal industries is still textile production. Most textile mills are located in the northwestern part of the state. The manufacture of chemicals is the state's chief income producer. Other leading industries include non-electrical machinery such as shovels, rakes, and other farming tools, paper and paper products, and food and food products.

Back	Forward	Stop	Review	Home	Explore	Favorites	History

Chapter 4 ▶

Government

The capital of South Carolina is Columbia. South Carolina state government follows the federal government in that it is split into three branches: executive, legislative, and judicial. The state government is governed under a constitution that was adopted in 1895. The constitution has had hundreds of amendments since its adoption.

▷ Executive

The executive branch is comprised of the governor, the lieutenant governor, and seven constitutional officers. Each serves a four-year term. The governor serves a four-year term and is elected by the people. Governors may not serve more than two terms in a row.

▷ South Carolina Legislature

There are one hundred seventy members of the South Carolina legislature. The South Carolina legislature is made up of two parts—the senate and the house of representatives. There are forty-six members in the senate and one hundred twenty-four members in the house of representatives. These two governing bodies, the senate and house of representatives, are referred to as the general assembly. Members of the house serve for two years; senators serve for four years.

The legislative branch has the greatest power over day-to-day affairs. It controls finances, and appointments to the state courts and to boards, commissions, and agencies. The

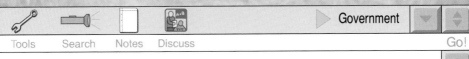
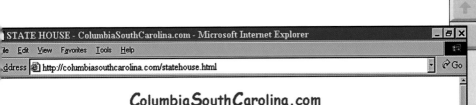

STATE HOUSE - ColumbiaSouthCarolina.com - Microsoft Internet Explorer

File   Edit   View   Favorites   Tools   Help

Address http://columbiasouthcarolina.com/statehouse.html   Go

ColumbiaSouthCarolina.com

South Carolina's STATE HOUSE

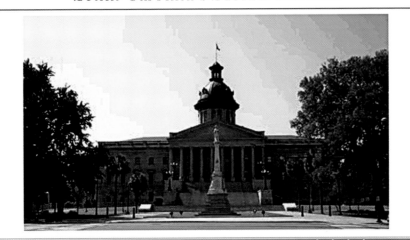

Internet

▲ *South Carolina's state house is located in the state capital of Columbia.*

county is the unit of local government. South Carolina has forty-six counties, most of which are governed by a council or board of commissioners. Many counties also have a county administrator or manager.

South Carolina elects two senators and six representatives to the U.S. Congress. The state has eight electoral votes in presidential elections.

▷ Judicial Branch

Judicial authority is contained in the state supreme court. It is made up of the chief justice and four associate justices.

The justices serve ten-year terms and are also elected by the legislature. The thirty-one judges of the circuit court, the main trial court, are elected by the legislature to six-year terms.

▷ Shifts in Politics

In local, state, and national elections, South Carolina had traditionally been a stronghold of the Democratic party. Since the 1950s, however, the Republican party has been gaining strength. In 1975, the state's first Republican governor in one hundred years took office. In presidential elections, South Carolina cast its electoral votes for the Democratic nominees from 1880 until 1948. That year, the state supported its own governor, Strom Thurmond (1902–2003), running as the candidate of the States Rights party. Thurmond won election to the U.S. Senate as a Democrat in 1956 but changed his party affiliation to Republican in 1964.

Since the 1960s, Republicans have held the edge in South Carolina's presidential voting. James Edwards became the state's first Republican governor in 1979.

◁ Strom Thurmond, shown here with his family, was born on December 5, 1902 in Edgefield, South Carolina. After serving as a state senator and governor, Thurmond was elected to the U.S. Senate in 1954.

History

Before European colonists settled in South Carolina, American Indians occupied the land. The American Indian population continued to grow until there were about ten thousand American Indians living in the state. There were at least twenty-nine tribes. Places such as Cherokee Falls in Cherokee County and the Stono River in Charleston were named after some of these tribes,

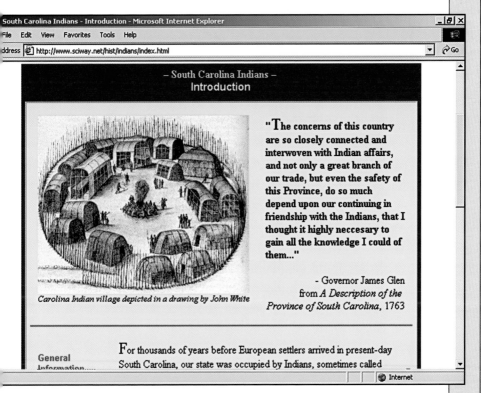

▲ This image depicts what the structure of an American Indian village looked like in the area that is now South Carolina.

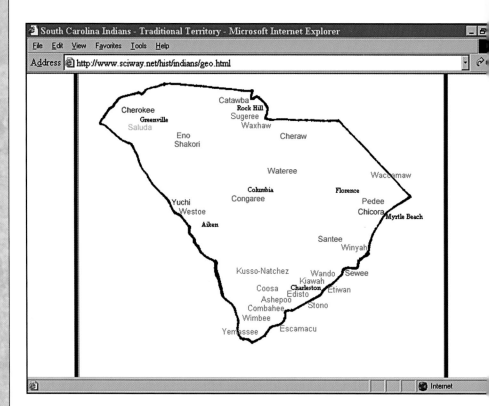

▲ *Here is a map of where South Carolina's tribes originally lived before the arrival of European settlers.*

showing the important role the American Indians played in the state's history.

When the European colonists came, they took over the land and gradually forced the American Indians out. The American Indian population started to decrease. The Europeans were carriers of the smallpox disease, which killed many of the American Indians. The American Indians had never been exposed to smallpox before and had no immunity to it. Meanwhile, the American Indians began fighting with the white settlers over the land, leading to the deaths of more of their people.

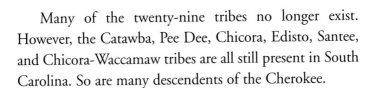

Many of the twenty-nine tribes no longer exist. However, the Catawba, Pee Dee, Chicora, Edisto, Santee, and Chicora-Waccamaw tribes are all still present in South Carolina. So are many descendents of the Cherokee.

Explorers

Francisco Gordillo was sent to explore the Americas for Spain in 1521. Gordillo is thought to have landed in either Florida or South Carolina. A failed attempt to colonize the area for Spain took place in 1526.

In 1562, Jean Ribaut sailed to the Americas to settle the South Carolina region for France. Ribaut established a Huguenot (a French Reformed religion) settlement on Parris Island in Port Royal Sound, but it was short lived.

The English eventually established the first successful colony in 1607. The colony they settled was Virginia, which became the first of England's thirteen American colonies. Since this colonization was successful, King Charles I started looking at the surrounding lands. He gave the land south of Virginia to Sir Robert Heath. Because the king gave him this land, Heath named it "Carolana" (Land of Charles). Heath attempted to settle the area that was to become South Carolina but his effort failed.

Under King Charles II, Carolana was renamed Carolina. In 1663, the king granted the land to eight landlords called *lords proprietors* to take care of the land. His intent was that people who moved to Carolina would pay them rent.

The eight proprietors found more than a hundred people from England willing to move to the Carolina colony. They set sail in the summer of 1669. The settlers arrived in March 1670. They built Carolina's first town.

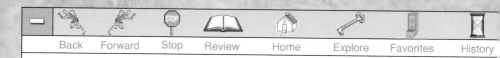
They called it Charles Town, later renamed Charleston. Charleston was South Carolina's only permanent town for forty years.

▷ Colonial Times

In colonial times, the settlers survived by learning to farm. They grew corn and other crops. Soon it became apparent that they needed more. The American Indians introduced rice to the colonists, and taught them how to grow it.

Rice became a major food product. The settlers were even able to sell the rice in Europe. This became their first cash crop. Because so many people were buying the rice, the farmers needed more help in growing the rice. The

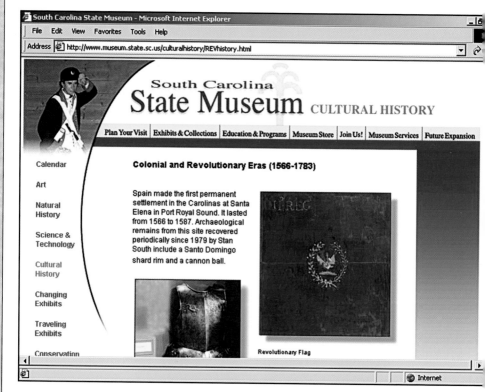

For many years, South Carolinians battled the American Indians for land.

farmers bought African slaves to help them with the cultivation of the rice. Soon these farmers built large plantations. The slaves worked on these plantations.

By 1710, there were more blacks than whites in the colony. The slaves were often treated poorly by the whites. It was not an easy life. They worked long and hard. Although they had shelter, it was not comfortable. They did not have nice things to eat.

From 1739 to 1740, some slaves fought with the white South Carolinians landowners. About sixty slaves and thirty white people were killed during this time. This was called the Stono Rebellion. The Stono battle began along the Stono River.

American Indians Fight Back

The American Indians began to raid the settlers as well. They felt the white colonists were taking over their land. As the Carolina town of Beaufort was being founded in 1710, American Indians attacked the white colonists. Then, from 1715 to 1717, the American Indians fought a bloody battle with the colonists. This was known as the Yamasee War. Both sides suffered many losses. In the end, the white Carolinians won that battle.

Besides the internal fighting with the African slaves and the American Indians, the colonists also fought pirates. At that time, because the South Carolina colony became rich from the sale of rice, pirates were attracted to the area. The most notorious pirate was called Blackbeard. His real name was Edward Teach. He was called Blackbeard because he had a long black beard, which he tied with colored ribbons. He robbed ships off the Carolina coast in 1717. He ended up robbing eight or nine ships before he was stopped. Another infamous

pirate was Stede Bonnet. He made people "walk the plank," or jump into the ocean to die. Like several other pirates, Bonnet was captured and hung.

▷ Separate Colonies

In the early-1700s, the Carolinas were split into two sections. The two sections became North and South Carolina. Although the Carolinas were wealthy from the sale of rice, they did not make the lords proprietors as rich as they wanted. The lords proprietors sold South Carolina back to the king in 1721. They also decided to sell North Carolina back to the king in 1729. Under the rule of the king, South

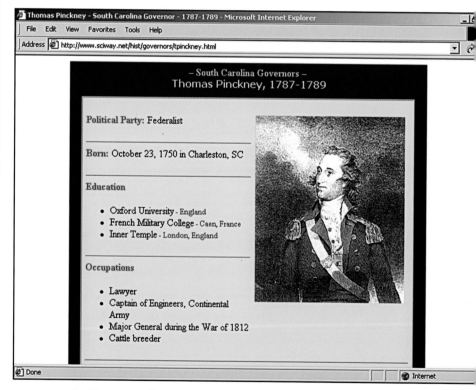

▲ Thomas Pinckney was born in Charleston, South Carolina, in 1750. He served as governor of South Carolina from 1787 until 1789. In 1778, he presided over the state to ratify its constitution.

Carolina did better. More and more people settled inland and new towns were built. Orangeburg and Florence were the next towns to be established.

The colony's first successful newspaper began in 1732. It was called the *South Carolina Gazette*. Then in 1736, one of America's first playhouses opened in Charleston—the Dock Street Theater.

Eliza Lucas Pinckney

Eliza Lucas Pinckney made two major contributions to South Carolina history. Eliza was born in 1722 on the Caribbean Island of Antigua. First, she made a major impact on the state's economy when she created a high-quality blue dye from the indigo plant. The blue dye was in great demand from the English who used it to make their uniforms and dress coats. This became a new source for South Carolina's struggling economy. Pinckney taught others how to grow it, and she became a wealthy woman. In 1989, Eliza Lucas Pinckney was inducted into the South Carolina Business Hall of Fame. She was the first woman so honored.

Secondly, Eliza made another major impact on South Carolina when she married a man named Charles Pinckney in 1744 and had four children. Charles Pinckney was a Chief Justice of the Province. Two of their sons became national figures: Charles Cotesworth Pinckney was a general in the Revolutionary War and a signer of the United States Constitution. Thomas Pinckney was a general and a famous diplomat. He served as United States minister to Britain, and Spain.

The Revolutionary War Era

Following the French and Indian War in 1763, England needed money. The English felt the colonists should pay

for their part in the war. They started to tax the colonists on paint and tea among other commodities.

The English used the Stamp Act of 1765 as a way to tax the colonists. The colonists were infuriated by this act and retaliated by rioting and wreaking havoc in the streets. These actions brought a repeal of the act, but many new taxes were drawn up to take its place.

The colonists were again angered by these new taxes. Their major complaint was that there was no representation of the colonists in the English Parliament. The colonists soon came up with the famous chant "Taxation without representation is tyranny."

▶ American Revolution

This conflict between the colonists and England resulted in the Revolutionary War. The war began on April 19, 1775, in Massachusetts. About twenty-five thousand South Carolinians participated in the war.

Charleston was England's first target. The English ships landed in Charleston in June 1776. The people of Charleston sprung into action. As the South Carolinians defended the town, Colonel William Moultrie and his men started building a fort to protect the town as the enemy approached Sullivan's Island. Palmetto logs were used to build the fort.

On June 28, 1776, Fort Moultrie was bombarded with cannonballs. The fort did not fall. The palmetto logs were strong enough to withstand the cannonballs. During the battle, the South Carolina flag was shot down. One of the patriots, Sergeant William Jasper ran out of the fort, picked up the flag and raised it to fly above Fort Moultrie. The English lost this battle.

This was a pivotal point for the Americans. On July 4, 1776, six days later, America declared its independence from

Britain. Four men signed the Declaration of Independence for South Carolina. They are Edward Rutledge, Thomas Heyward, Jr., Thomas Lynch, Jr., and Arthur Middleton.

Following the signing of the Declaration, freedom did not come easily to the Americans. Britain continued to fight. In 1780, Charleston was attacked again. This time, the Americans lost. The British continued its attempt to take over South Carolina but only succeeded in taking over a small portion of the state.

Famous Patriots

Francis Marion was one of South Carolina's best-remembered patriots. He was nicknamed the Swamp Fox

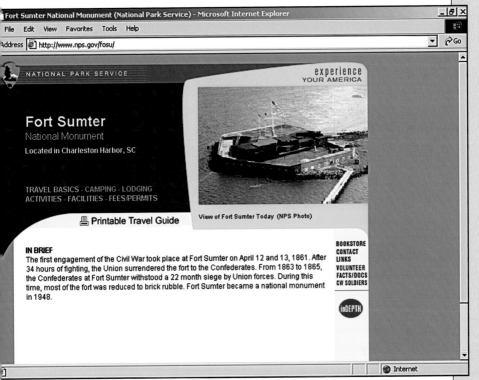

Fort Sumter is where the first engagement of the Civil War took place between April 12 and April 13, 1861. After thirty-four hours, the Union Army surrendered. In 1948, Fort Sumter became a national monument.

because he and his men would hide in the swamps of eastern South Carolina and make surprise attacks on the enemy. Although he was only five feet tall and limped, his successful surprise attacks on the enemy soon caused the enemy to fear him. Marion's role helped turn the tide of the war in the South.

Thomas Sumter followed in the footsteps of Francis Marion. He also formed a guerrilla band to fight the British. Most of his raids were in the central part of South Carolina. The "gamecock of the Revolution," as Sumter was called, defeated the British at Hanging Rock, participated in the war at Fishing Creek, and took part in a raid on the British post at Rocky Mount. He then won again at the Battle of Blackstock. Fort Sumter in Charleston is named after him.

Andrew Pickens was another famous patriot of South Carolina during the Revolutionary War. After he rose to brigadier general, he took part in the victories at Kettle Creek (1779) and at Cowpens, Augusta, and Eutaw Springs (all in 1781).

Because of their dedication to protecting and saving South Carolina from the hands of the British, all three had counties named after them in the respective areas where they fought.

▶ End of the War

Three big battles finally ended the Revolutionary War. The Battle of Camden (August 16, 1780), the Battle at Kings Mountain (October 7, 1780) and the Battle of Cowpens (January 17, 1781) were three crucial battles that helped end the Revolutionary War. Although the Americans lost the Battle of Camden, the battles at Kings Mountain and Cowpens were successes that broke

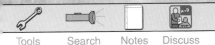

England's spirit. In 1783, the peace treaty was signed. The United States was finally free from England.

On May 23, 1788, South Carolina became the eighth state to join the Union.

▶ Slavery and Civil War

With the invention of the cotton gin by Eli Whitney in 1793, South Carolina's economy grew rapidly. The cotton gin allowed the farmers to "pick" the cotton (separating the seeds from the fibers) almost 50 percent faster than by hand. Cotton became a major cash crop.

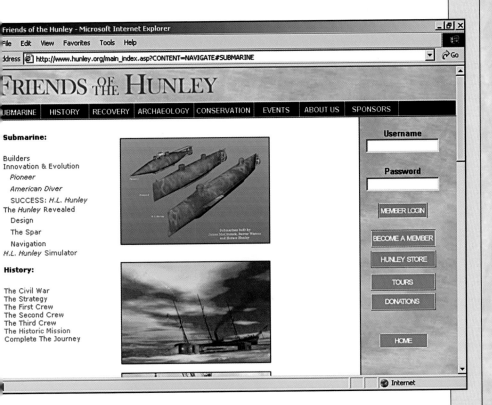

▲ The H.L. Hunley, a Confederate submarine, disappeared off the coast of South Carolina in 1864. It was the first submarine to be used successfully in warfare.

Although the cotton gin produced cotton more quickly, the farmers needed more workers to keep up with the demands of the cotton. Most of the people they used to work the land were African slaves. By the mid-1800s, the slaves made up more than half of the population of the state.

A conflict arose between the North and South concerning the use of slaves and other issues. Most of the northern states had already ended slavery. The South disagreed. They felt that each state had the right to decide for themselves on these kinds of issues. South Carolinian John C. Calhoun also believed this so he created the theory of nullification, by which a state could reject any federal law it considered a violation of its rights.

On December 20, 1860, angry over the issues of having restrictions on free trade and ending slavery, the South Carolinians seceded from the Union. Eleven Southern states followed. These eleven states were called the Confederate States of America. The Confederates fired the first shots on the morning of April 12, 1861 on Fort Sumter beginning the Civil War.

During the Civil War, the Confederacy produced the world's first successful submarine, the *Hunley*. The *Hunley* was the first to sink an enemy ship, the Union ship *Housatonic*. No other submarines sank an enemy ship until World War I. The *Hunley* has been recovered and was taken to Charleston on Tuesday, August 8, 2000.[1]

The Civil War ended on April 9, 1865 with the Union (North) declaring victory over the Confederate Army (South). Soon after the war was ended, the Thirteenth Amendment to the U.S. Constitution was passed, formally ending slavery.

During the war, much of South Carolina had been destroyed. Farms and industries had been wiped out.

Cities and towns had been burned. Roads and railroads were in bad shape. South Carolina was in desperate need of repair.

Reconstruction Period

The Civil War, particularly General William T. Sherman's March to the Sea in early 1865, left South Carolina in total devastation. Plantations, farms, and most of the city of Columbia were destroyed by fire during this march. The economic framework of the state was totally destroyed. The monies from the Confederacy no longer had any value.

It was time to rebuild the state. The state received help from some Northerners. These Northerners came down and helped repair roads, planted crops on farms, and helped rebuild buildings. Not all of the Northerners who

▲ *South Carolinians hope that the sun has set over an era of economic instability and racial strife.*

came down to help were good people, though. These people were called carpetbaggers. Even though the carpetbaggers came down to help, the intentions of some were not good. They overcharged for their services. They were called carpetbaggers because they carried a carpetbag when they came down to help. This period of rebuilding and reorganizing the South was called the Reconstruction Period. It lasted nearly ten years following the Civil War.

By the beginning of the twentieth century, the effects of the Civil War on the state's economy were finally starting to recover. The textile industry was the first to develop, then in the years that followed, other manufacturers moved into the state. These manufacturers provided jobs and economic stability.

The second half of the twentieth century also brought enormous change in the status of African American South Carolinians. The civil rights movement of the 1960s brought a relatively peaceful end to segregation and legal discrimination. The most serious incident of this period occurred in 1968 at Orangeburg, where state police shot three African-American protesters. Two years later, three African Americans were elected to the state legislature. Many others have subsequently served in state and local offices.

In more recent years high-tech industries have brought jobs to South Carolinians as well. The state has made technology education a priority. The state requires its school teachers to undergo technology training. South Carolina ranks among the leaders in providing Internet access to its students. By the start of the twenty-first century, South Carolina was surely a state on the rise.

Chapter Notes

Chapter 1. The Palmetto State

1. U.S. Census Bureau, "South Carolina," *State and County QuickFacts,* May 7, 2003, <http://quickfacts.census.gov/qfd/states/45000.html> (May 20, 2003).

2. Slicker, "Visit Historic Boone Plantation and Gardens," *Boone Hall Plantation,* n.d., <http://www.boonehallplantation.com/> (May 20, 2003).

3. State Library of North Carolina Webteam, "Andrew Jackson," *State Library of North Carolina: North Carolina Encyclopedia,* March 5, 1998, <http://statelibrary.dcr.state.nc.us/nc/bio/public/jackson.htm#Childhood> (May 20, 2003).

4. The Byrnes Scholars, "The James F. Byrnes Scholarships: Statesman, Jurist, Humanitarian," *The Byrnes Scholarships,* 1998–2003, <http://www.byrnesscholars.org/history/jfbsjh.htm> (May 20, 2003).

Chapter 2. Land and Climate

1. Microsoft Corporation, "South Carolina," *Reference With Encarta,* © 1993–2003 Microsoft Corporation, <http://encarta.msn.com/encnet/refpages/RefArticle.aspx?refid=761571763&para=47#p47> (May 20, 2003).

2. NSTATE, "The Geography of South Carolina," *South Carolina,* May 4, 2003, <http://www.netstate.com/states/geography/sc_geography.htm> (May 20, 2003).

Chapter 3. Economy

1. South Carolina Department of Agriculture, "Agriculture and Forestry," *South Carolina Agriculture and Forestry,* n.d., <http://www.scda.state.sc.us/consumerinformation/scagandforestry/scagandforestry.htm> (May 20, 2003).

2. South Carolina Department of Agriculture, "Little-Known South Carolina Agricultural Facts," *South Carolina Agriculture and Forestry,* n.d., <http://www.scda.state.sc.us/consumerinformation/agfacts/agfacts.htm> (May 20, 2003).

3. South Carolina Department of Agriculture, "Agriculture and Forestry."

4. Ibid.

5. Ibid.

6. Ibid.

Chapter 5. History

1. Dr. Frank Oliver Clark, "The *Hunley* Has Been Recovered," *The First Modern Submarine, and the First to Sink an EnemyShip!,* October 15, 2000, <http://sciway3.net/clark/civilwar/navy.html> (May 20, 2003).

Further Reading

Buchanan, John. *The Road to Guilford Courthouse: The American Revolution in the Carolinas.* New York: John Wiley & Sons, Inc., 1997.

Capstone Press Staff, *South Carolina.* Minnetonka, Minn.: Capstone Press, Incorporated, 1997.

Chappell, Ruth Paterson. *All 'Bout Charleston.* Orangeburg, S.Car.: Sandlapper Publishing Company, Inc., 1998.

Edgar, Walter B. *Partisans and Redcoats: the Southern Conflict that Turned the Tide of the American Revolution.* New York: HarperCollins, 2001.

Feinstein, Stephen. *Andrew Jackson: A MyReportLinks.com Book.* Berkeley Heights, N.J.: MyReportLinks.com Books, 2002.

Fradin, Dennis Brindell. *South Carolina.* Danbury, Conn.: Children's Press, 1992.

Haskins, James. *Jesse Jackson: Civil Rights Activist.* Berkeley Heights, N.J.: Enslow Publishers, Inc., 2000.

Hoffman, Nancy. *South Carolina.* Tarrytown, N.Y.: Marshall Cavendish Corporation, 2000.

Kavanagh, James. *South Carolina Birds.* Blaine, Wash.: Waterford Press, Limited, 1999.

Stein, R. Conrad. *South Carolina.* Danbury, Conn.: Children's Press, 1999.

Thompson, Kathleen. *South Carolina.* Austin, Tex.: Raintree Steck-Vaughn Publishers, 1996.

Index